AMERICAN PRESIDENTS

ABRAHAM LINCOLN

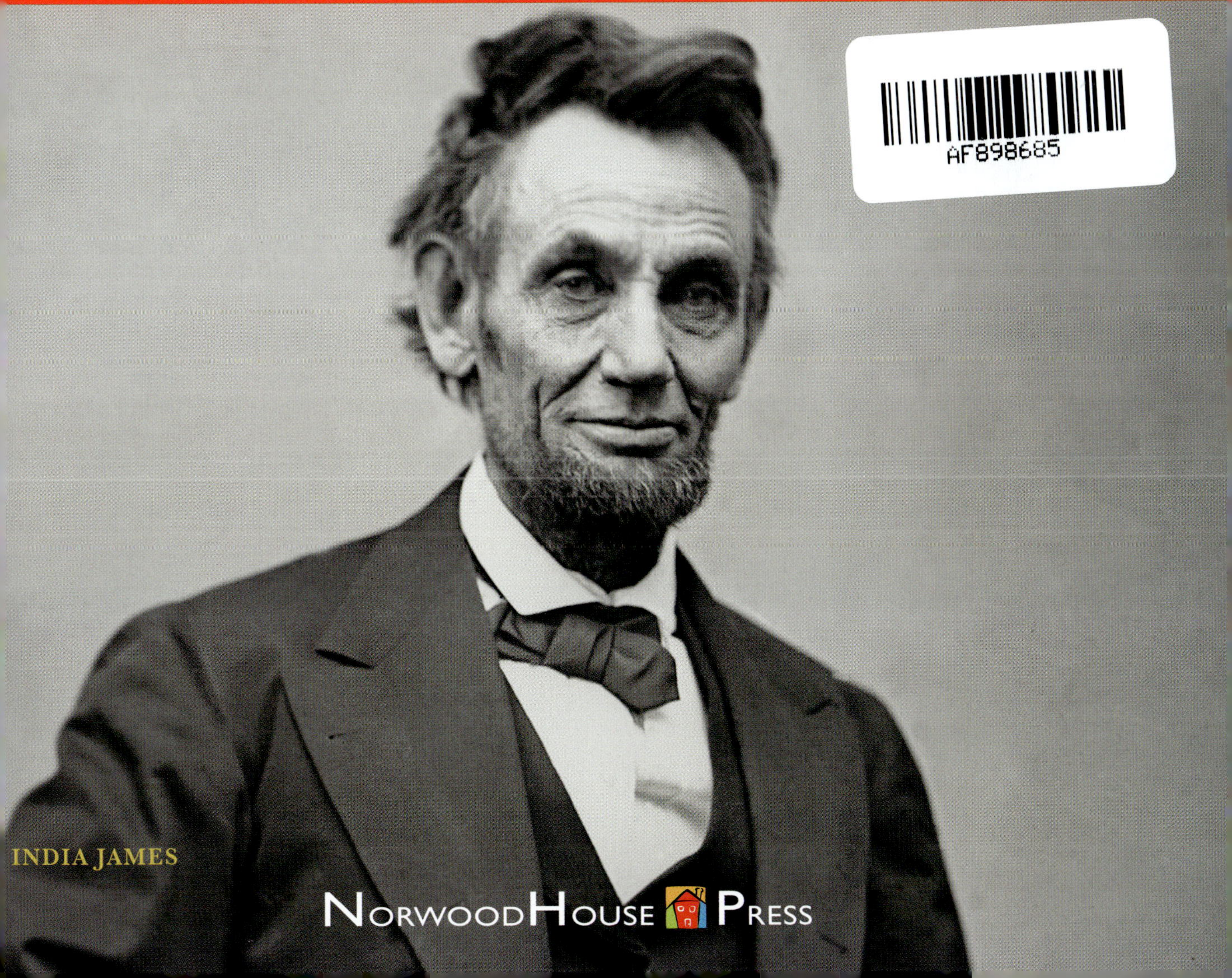

INDIA JAMES

NorwoodHouse Press

Cataloging-in-Publication Data

Names: James, India.
Title: Abraham Lincoln / India James.
Description: Buffalo, NY : Norwood House Press, 2027. | Series: American presidents | Includes glossary and index.
Identifiers: ISBN 9781978579699 (pbk.) | ISBN 9781978579705 (library bound) | ISBN 9781978579712 (ebook)
Subjects: LCSH: Lincoln, Abraham, 1809-1865--Juvenile literature. | Presidents--United States--Biography--Juvenile literature. | Presidents--Biography--Juvenile literature.
Classification: LCC E457.905 J36 2027 | DDC 973.7092--dc23

Published in 2027 by
Norwood House Press
2544 Clinton Street
Buffalo, NY 14224

Designer: Rhea Magaro
Editor: Kim Thompson

Photo credits: Cover, pp. 1, 9, 12 Everett Collection/Shutterstock.com; pp. 5-7, 13-15, 17, 18 Library of Congress; pp. 10, 20 Wikipedia; p. 11 The White House; p. 21 Andy Sutherland/Shutterstock.com;

Printed in the United States of America

CPSIA compliance information: Batch #CSNHP27: For further information contact Norwood House Press at 1-800-237-9932.

TABLE OF CONTENTS

Early Years

Abraham Lincoln was born on February 12, 1809. He lived in a log cabin near Hodgenville, Kentucky.

The family was poor. Abe's mother and father could not read or write. When Abe was nine years old, his mother died.

Abe did not go to school very often. He went for a few weeks at a time before he had to stop and help his family. Altogether, he attended school for less than one year.

But young Abe loved to read. After his father remarried, his stepmother encouraged him to read. He taught himself about the world by reading books.

Building a Career

Abe tried many jobs. He worked on a boat in the Mississippi River. He built fences. He worked at a post office.

People recognized how smart Abe was. When he was 25, Abe was elected to the Illinois **legislature**. He served four **terms** in all. Abe liked working with the law. He read law books. He passed a test to become a lawyer.

In 1842, Abe married Mary Todd.

Abe was elected to represent Illinois in the United States **Congress**. He did not win reelection, so he worked as a lawyer.

Presidency

There were millions of enslaved people in the southern U.S. Abe thought **slavery** was wrong. He made public speeches against it.

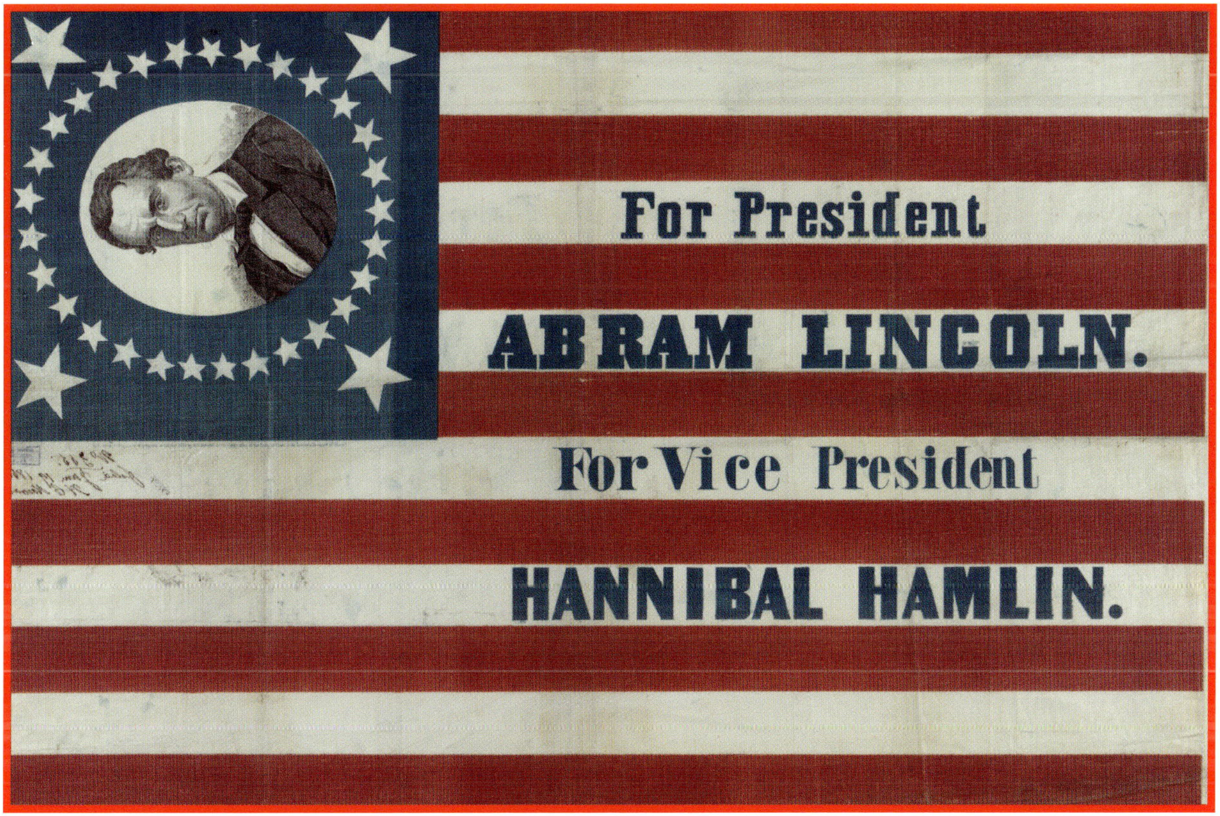

People liked what Abe said. They convinced him to run for president. In 1860, Abraham Lincoln was elected the 16th president of the United States.

Southern states **seceded** to form their own country. President Lincoln wanted to keep the U.S. together and end slavery. In 1861, the Civil War began. The North fought the South.

In 1863, Abe signed the Emancipation Proclamation. The document said that enslaved people in the South were free.

After a terrible Civil War battle, Abe gave a famous speech called the Gettysburg Address. He said that people must keep fighting to save the **union**. He said, "Government of the people, by the people, for the people, shall not perish from the earth."

Abe was elected to a second term as president. The North won the Civil War. Many southerners were angry, including one man who **assassinated** the president in a theater. Abraham Lincoln died on April 15, 1865.

Legacy

Abraham Lincoln is remembered as one of the greatest U.S. presidents. He ended slavery. He kept the country together.

The Lincoln Memorial in Washington, D.C., honors the great president. It is one of the most visited **monuments** in the nation's capital.

Glossary

assassinated (uh-SAS-uh-nay-ted): murdered someone who is well-known or important

Congress (CON-gruhs): the part of the U.S. government that makes laws and that includes the House of Representatives and the Senate

legislature (LEJ-is-lay-chur): a group of people who have the power to make or change laws for a state or country

monuments (MAHN-yuh-muhnts): statues or structures built to remind people of an important person or event

seceded (si-SEED-ed): left a group; withdrew from a country to form a new country

slavery (SLAY-vur-ee): a system in which people are kidnapped, kept against their will, and made to work without pay or rights; slavery of Black people was legal in the United States before the Civil War

terms (turmz): definite or set periods of time; American presidents are elected to terms that last four years

union (YOON-yuhn): the group of states that makes up the United States of America

Thinking Questions

1. How did Abraham Lincoln learn as a child?
2. Give examples of some jobs that Abe tried.
3. What speech did Abe give to encourage people to unite the country?
4. How many times was Abe elected president?
5. What is the Lincoln Memorial?

Index

About the Author

India James writes about science, technology, math, and history for young readers. She loves learning new things while writing books. India lives in Ohio with her family.